Plastic

Holly Wallace

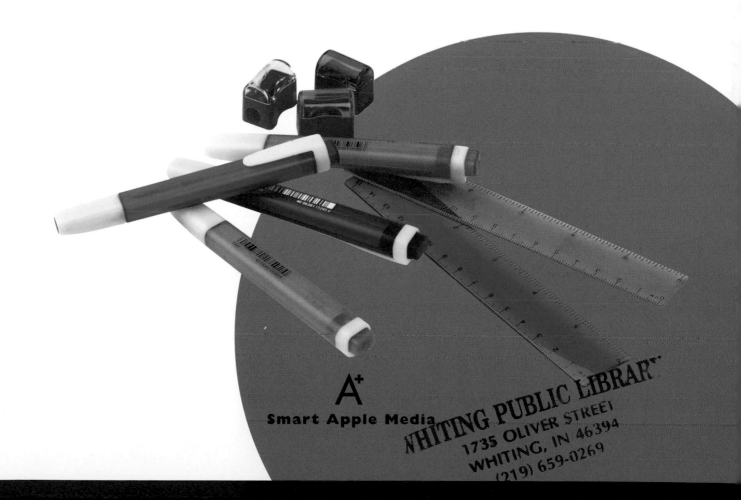

A⁺
Smart Apple Media

This book has been published in cooperation with Franklin Watts.

Series designed and created for Franklin Watts by Painted Fish Ltd., Art director: Jonathan Hair, Designer: Rita Storey, Editor: Fiona Corbridge

Picture credits:
Corbis p. 22 (left); General Mill Supply Co. p. 27; istockphoto.com p. 8, p. 20 (top), p. 23 (top), p. 26; Tudor Photography pp. 6–9, pp. 10–20, p. 21 (bottom), p. 22 (right), p. 23 (bottom), p. 24, p. 25.

Cover images: Tudor Photography, Banbury

Published in the United States by Smart Apple Media
2140 Howard Drive West, North Mankato, Minnesota 56003

Library of Congress Cataloging-in-Publication Data

Wallace, Holly, 1961-
Plastic / by Holly Wallace.
p. cm. – (How we use materials)
Includes index.
ISBN-13: 978-1-59920-005-7
1. Plastics—Juvenile literature. 2. Building materials—Juvenile literature. I. Title.

TA455.P5W27 2007
620.1'923—dc22   2006029887

9 8 7 6 5 4 3 2 1

Contents

Words in **bold** are
in the glossary.

What is plastic?

Plastic is a **material**. We use plastic to make many different things.

Look around you. How many things can you see that are made from plastic?

There are plastic bags, pens, rulers, and pencil sharpeners.

Plastic is a useful material because it is light, strong, and **waterproof**. The cover and handle on this umbrella are plastic.

Plastic is cheap to make, so things such as these plastic bathroom objects do not cost as much to buy.

Plastic keywords
Material
Waterproof
Strong
Light

7

Where does plastic come from?

Plastic is not a **natural** material. It is made in factories from **chemicals**.

Most of the chemicals come from **oil**. The oil comes from under the sea or underground.

● People drill for oil from oil rigs.

In the factory, the chemicals are used to make tiny **chips** of plastic. The chips are now ready to be made into different plastic objects.

The chips are heated up so that they melt and become a liquid. The liquid plastic is poured into **molds** to make different shapes, such as these baskets. The plastic cools and becomes hard.

Plastic keywords

Chemicals

Oil

Molds

What is plastic like?

There are lots of different kinds of plastic. We use them for many different jobs.

 These boxes and this cell phone are made of strong plastic. They do not break easily.

Some plastic is soft and easy to **bend**. These drinking straws are made from bendable plastic.

Plastic can be made in many colors. We use colored plastic to make toys.

Plastic keywords
Soft
Bendable
Colored

Plastic in buildings

Plastic is strong and waterproof. It is a good material to use in buildings.

Plastic pipes carry used water from baths and sinks.

Other pipes help rain to drain from buildings. Plastic is a good material to use for pipes because it lasts a long time and is waterproof.

People sometimes make window frames from plastic instead of wood. This is because plastic does not **rot** like wood does. These frames are made from a plastic called **PVC**.

Pipes that go under the ground are often made from plastic instead of metal. This is because plastic does not **rust** like metal does.

Plastic keywords

PVC

Plastic in the home

Lots of the things in your home are made from plastic. How many can you find?

Some plastic is thick and strong. It is made so that it will be **durable**.

Durable plastic is good for making things that are used a lot, such as vacuum cleaners and CD players.

Some plastic is **transparent**—this means we can see through it. Transparent plastic also lets light shine through it. It is useful for things such as the end of this flashlight.

Plastic can be thin. This shower curtain is made from a thin, bendable sheet of plastic. It is waterproof.

Plastic keywords

Durable
Transparent
Thin

15

Plastic in the kitchen

Plastic is very useful in the kitchen. It is hard to break and safe to use for **containers** that hold food and drink.

● This bowl is plastic. Plastic is waterproof and does not let liquid pass through it. Bendable plastics are good for making sports bottles.

Heat cannot flow through plastic well. So when people use plastic **utensils** to stir hot food, the handle does not get hot.

This plastic coffee pot will keep liquids inside it hot.

Garbage cans are often made of plastic because plastic is easy to clean.

Plastic keywords

Safe
Clean

Plastic packages

Many different kinds of plastic are used to make **packages**.

Plastic packages hold and **protect** the things we buy at the store.

Some packages are transparent to show us what is inside. The plastic can also be **printed** with words and pictures.

● We use thin sheets of soft, stretchy plastic for wrapping food. This keeps it fresh and clean.

● A light plastic called **polystyrene** is used to make takeout containers. It helps keep the food warm.

Plastic keywords
Packages
Polystyrene
Stretchy

Plastic in the garden

Plastic is very good for making things that we use outdoors, too.

- Some garden tools are made from plastic because it is strong and does not rust.

- Plastic is good for watering cans because it is waterproof and light.

Flowerpots can be made from clay or plastic. A plastic flower pot lasts longer than a clay pot and does not break as easily.

Plastic keywords

Lasts long
Flexible

This wading pool is made from thin plastic. It is flexible so that you can blow it up. When the air is let out, the pool can be folded up and put away.

21

Plastic in clothes

Did you know that some of the clothes you wear are made from plastic?

- Plastic can be spun into long threads called **fibers**. Then the fibers are **woven** together to make pieces of fabric.

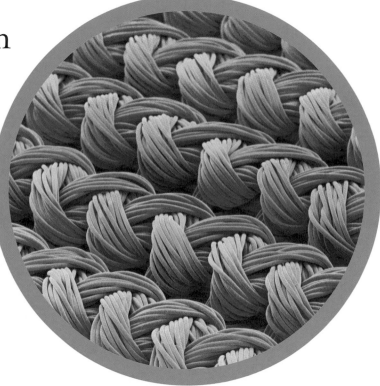

- **Acrylic** and **polyester** are plastic fabrics. These socks are made from acrylic.

This fleece top is made from polyester. The fabric is warm and does not **wrinkle**. It does not stretch out of shape.

We need plastic boots on rainy days. Because they are waterproof, we can jump in puddles and our feet will not get wet.

Plastic keywords

Fibers
Woven
Fabric

23

Plastic in vehicles

Because plastic is light and strong it is used to make parts of cars, bikes, and airplanes.

- Plastic is easy to make into shapes, such as the different parts of this car.

● Transparent plastic is used instead of glass for things such as lights on cars and bikes. Glass can hurt people if it breaks. It is safer to use plastic.

● The wings and body of this small airplane are made from plastic. This helps keep the plane light so it will fly easily.

Recycling plastic

Plastic is a very useful material because it does not rot. But this causes problems.

When we throw plastic things away, they last forever. This makes lots of garbage.

Plastic bottles do not rot in the ground.

Some plastic can be melted and used again. Then it is made into chips. The chips are made into new plastic things. This is called **recycling**.

If plastic is recycled then factories do not have to use more oil to make new plastic.

This traffic cone is made from recycled plastic.

Plastic keywords

Garbage
Recycling
Melting

Glossary

Bend Make into a curved shape.

Chemicals Special substances used to do many jobs, including making plastic.

Chips Small pieces.

Containers Boxes used for storing food and other things.

Durable A material which is tough and strong, and lasts for a long time.

Fibers Long, thin pieces of a material.

Material Something from which other objects can be made.

Molds Specially shaped containers that liquid plastic is poured into to make plastic objects in those shapes.

Natural Something that comes from the earth, plants, or animals.

Oil Thick black liquid found underground or under the sea. It is used for fuel and to help make many other things.

Packages The wrappers or containers used to store the things we buy.

Polystyrene A type of light plastic.

Printed Marked with words or pictures.

Protect Stop things from getting spoiled or harmed.

PVC A type of plastic called polyvinyl chloride.

Recycling Using a material again.

Rot When a material becomes soft and crumbly.

Rust When some types of metal get wet, a reddish-brown substance forms on them called rust. Rust eats away metal and makes it weaker.

Substance The material that a thing is made up of.

Transparent Clear or see-through.

Utensils Spoons, scoops, and other tools used in the kitchen.

Waterproof Does not let water pass through.

Woven Weaving fibers together (threading them in, out, and around each other) to make a fabric or cloth.

Wrinkle Make lines or folds in something.

Index